junie b. jones®
and
Her Big Fat Mouth

Junie B. Jones and Her Big Fat Mouth by Barbara Park

Text copyright © 1993 by Barbara Park
Cover art and interior illustrations copyright © 1993 by Denise Brunkus
All rights reserved.

This bilingual edition was published by Longtail Books in 2021 by arrangement with Barbara Park c/o Writers House LLC through KCC(Korea Copyright Center Inc.), Seoul.

ISBN 979-11-91343-10-6 14740

Longtail Books

junie b. jones®
and
Her Big Fat Mouth

by BARBARA PARK

illustrated by
Denise Brunkus

Contents

1. Punishment   7

2. The Cop and Dr. Smiley   20

3. Me and My Big Fat Mouth   30

4. Dumb Ollie   40

5. Shining   48

6. Tingling   58

7. Jobs and Jobs   64

8. Gus Vallony   78

1
Punishment

My name is Junie B. Jones. The B **stand**s for Beatrice. **Except** I don't like Beatrice. I just like B and **that's all.**

I go to **kindergarten.** My room is named Room Nine. There are lots of **rule**s in that place.

Like no shouting.

And no running in the **hall.**

And no **butt**ing the other children in the

stomach with your head.

My teacher's name is Mrs.

She has another name, too. But I just like Mrs. and that's all.

Last week Mrs. **clap**ped her loud hands together. Then she made a **'nounce**ment to us.

A *'nouncement* is the school word for telling us something very important.

"Boys and girls. May I have your **attention**, please?" she said. "Today is going to be a special day in Room Nine. We're going to be talking about different **career**s you can have when you grow up."

"Yeah, only guess what?" I said. "I never even heard of that **dumb** word careers before. And so I won't know what the heck[1] we're talking about."

Mrs. made **squinty** eyes at me. "A career is a *job*, Junie B.," she said. "And please raise your hand before you speak."

Then Mrs. talked some more about careers. And she said Monday was going to be called Job Day. And everybody in Room Nine would come to school **dress**ed **up** like what kind of job they wanted to be.

After that, Room Nine was very excited. Except for not me. 'Cause I had a big problem, that's why.

"Yeah, only guess what?" I said. "I don't know what I want to be when I grow up. And so that means I can't come to school

---

1 **heck** '도대체', '젠장' 또는 '제기랄'이라는 뜻으로 당혹스럽거나 짜증스러운 감정을 강조하는 속어.

on Monday. And now I'll probably **flunk** kindergarten."

"**Hurray!**" shouted a **mean** boy named Jim.

I made a **fist** at him. "How'd you like a **knuckle** sandwich,^{2} you big fat Jim?" I shouted right back.

Mrs. came over to my table. She **bend**ed^3 down next to me.

"*Please*, Junie B. You simply must try to **control** yourself better in class. We've talked about this before, remember?"

"Yes," I said nicely. "Only I hate that

---

2 **knuckle sandwich** '다른 사람의 얼굴을 주먹으로 친다'라는 뜻의 속어적 표현.

3 **bended** (bent) 영어권 국가의 아이들이 동사의 과거형을 말할 때 모든 단어의 끝에 '-ed'를 붙이는 실수를 종종 한다. 이 책에 나오는 'blowed(blew)', 'hided(hid)' 등이 이와 같은 경우이다.

dumb guy."

Just then my bestest[4] friend Lucille—
who sits next to me—stood up and **fluff**ed
her **ruffly** dress.

"I always control myself, don't I,
Teacher?" she said. "That's because my
nanna taught me to act like a little lady.
And so Junie B. Jones should act more like
me."

I made a **growly** face at her. "I *do* act
like a little lady, you dumb bunny[5] Lucille!
And don't say that again, or I'll **knock** you
on your can.[6]"

Mrs. did a **frown** at me.

---

4 **bestest** 단어 'best(최고의)'를 강조한 비격식적인 표현. '최고로 좋은'
   이라는 뜻을 나타내며 어린아이가 주로 사용한다.
5 **dumb bunny** 좀 모자라거나 우직한 사람을 이르는 속어적 표현.

"Just **kid**ding," I said very quick.

Except for Mrs. kept on frowning. And then she gave me punishment.

Punishment is the school word for sitting at a big table all **by yourself.**

And everybody keeps on **staring** at you.

And it makes you feel like P.U.[7]

That's how come I put my head down on the table. And I **cover**ed it up with my arms.

'Cause punishment takes the **friendly right** out of you.

And so at **recess** I didn't speak to Lucille. And I didn't speak to my other

---

6 can '엉덩이'라는 뜻의 속어적 표현.
7 P.U. '어휴'라는 뜻으로 냄새나 악취가 날 때 혐오감 혹은 역겨움을 나타내는 표현. 여기에서는 역겨운 기분을 나타내기 위해 사용했다.

bestest friend named Grace, either.

I just sat down in the grass all by myself.

And I watched **Janitor** paint the **litter** cans.

And I played with a **stick** and an ant and that's all.

"I hate Room Nine," I said very **grump**ity.[8]

Except for just then I saw something very wonderful in the grass! And its name was two cherry Life Savers![9]

"Hey! I love those guys!" I said.

Then I quick picked one up. And I **blow**ed off the **germ**s. And I put it right in

---

8 **grumpity** 주니 B.가 만들어 낸 단어로 형용사 'grumpy(성격이 나쁜)' 를 활용하여 '투덜대며', '심술궂게'라는 뜻의 부사로 사용하였다.

9 **Life Savers** 라이프 세이버스. 미국에서 판매되는 고리 모양의 사탕으로 민트와 과일 맛이 난다.

my mouth.

"WAIT! DONT DO THAT!" shouted a loud voice at me. "**SPIT** THAT OUT RIGHT NOW!"

I turned my head.

It was Janitor! He was running at me **speedy** quick. His **jingly** keys were **jangling** all over the place.

"SPIT THAT OUT, I SAID!" he **yell**ed again.

And so then I spit the cherry Life Saver on the ground. 'Cause the guy was **scaring** me, that's why.

Janitor bended down next to me.

"I didn't mean to **frighten** you, sis,[10]"

---

10 **sis** '아가씨' 또는 '언니'라는 뜻으로 여자아이나 젊은 여자를 부를 때 사용하는 비격식적인 호칭이다.

he said. "But I **spot**ted a **bunch** of dirty candy in the grass. And I was going to clean it up when I finished painting."

He looked serious at me. "Don't you ever

eat anything you find on the ground. Do you hear? Not *ever*."

"But I blowed off the germs," I told him.

Janitor shook his head. "You can't blow germs off," he said. "Eating things that you find on the ground is very, very dangerous."

Then Janitor picked up the dangerous candy. "Now **run along** and play," he said.

I did a big **sigh**. "Yeah, only I can't," I said. "'Cause I **shot off my** big fat **mouth** in kindergarten. And then I got punishment. And now I hate my bestest friend Lucille."

Janitor smiled a little bit sad. "Life is hard sometimes, isn't it, sis?" he said.

I **bob**bed my head up and down. "Yes," I said. "Life is P.U."

Then Janitor **pat**ted my head and he walked away.

And so guess what?

I just like Janitor.

And that's all.

2
The Cop and Dr. Smiley

When we came in from **recess**, Mrs. was **clap**ping her loud hands together again.

"Boys and girls, please take your seats quickly! I've got a wonderful surprise for you!"

Then I got very excited inside my **stomach**! Because surprises are my most favorite[1] things in the whole world!

"IS IT JELLY DOUGHNUTS?[2]" I

shouted.

Mrs. put her finger to her **lips**. That means *be quiet*.

"YEAH, ONLY GUESS WHAT? JELLY DOUGHNUTS ARE MY MOST FAVORITE KIND OF DOUGHNUTS! **EXCEPT** I ALSO LIKE THE CREAMY KIND. AND THE CHOCOLATE KIND! AND THE KIND WITH RAINBOW SPRINKLES[3] ON THE TOP!"

After that, my mouth got very watering.

---

1 **most favorite** '가장 좋아하는'이라는 뜻을 지닌 비격식적인 표현. 원래는 단어 'favorite'이 '선호하는'이라는 의미를 나타내기 때문에 형용사의 최상급을 만드는 부사인 'most'를 잘 붙이지 않는다.

2 **jelly doughnut** 잼 도넛. 밀가루에 설탕이나 달걀 등을 섞어 고리 모양으로 만들고 기름에 튀긴 과자를 도넛이라 하는데, 이때 그 속을 과일 잼으로 채운 종류를 말한다.

3 **sprinkles** 스프링클. 쿠키나 케이크 등의 위에 뿌려서 장식하는 작은 막대 모양의 가루로 달달한 맛이 난다. 그중 여러 색이 섞인 것을 레인보우 스프링클(rainbow sprinkles)이라고 한다.

And some **drool** fell on the table.

I **wipe**d it up with my sweater **sleeve**.

Just then there was a **knock** on the door.

Mrs. hurried to open it.

"HEY! IT'S A COP!" I **holler**ed very excited.

The cop came into Room Nine.

He had on a blue shirt with a **shiny badge**. And shiny black **boot**s. And a shiny white **motorcycle** helmet.

Mrs. smiled. "Boys and girls, I would like you to meet my friend, **Officer** Mike. Officer Mike is a policeman. Who can tell me what policemen do?"

"I can!" I called out. "They **rest** people! 'Cause one time some cops rested a guy on my street. And so that means they made him take a **nap**, I think."

Just then that Jim I hate laughed very loud.

"They didn't *rest* him, stupid!" he hollered. "They *arrested* him! That means they took him to **jail**. And so your **neighbor**'s a dirty **rotten jailbird**!"

Then the other kids laughed too. And so I hided my head.

"Yeah, only I **hardly** even know the guy," I said to just myself.

After that, Officer Mike **took off** his shiny white helmet. And he told us some other **stuff** that cops do. Like give our dads **speed**ing **ticket**s. And rest drunk guys.

Also he let us play with his **handcuff**s and his shiny white helmet. Except for the helmet was very too big for my head. And it **cover**ed my whole **entire** eyes.

"HEY! WHO TURNED OUT THE LIGHTS?" I said.

'Cause that was a funny **joke**, of course.

Then another knock came at the door.

This time it was a lady in a long white

jacket. She was carrying a **giant** red **toothbrush**.

"Boys and girls, this is Dr. Smiley," said Mrs. "Dr. Smiley is a children's **dentist**."

Dr. Smiley hung up some posters of teeth. Then she talked all about Mr. **Tooth Decay**. And she said to **brush** our teeth at night. And also in the morning.

"Yeah, 'cause if you don't brush in the morning, your breath smells like **stink**," I said.

After that I showed Dr. Smiley my **wiggling** tooth.

"Losing baby teeth[4] is exciting, isn't it?" she asked.

---

4 **baby tooth** (pl. baby teeth) 유치 또는 젖니. 유아기 때 사용하는 이로, 7세경에 하나씩 빠져 영구치가 나온다.

"Yes," I said. "Except for I don't like the part where you cry and **spit blood**."

Dr. Smiley made a sick face. Then she passed out minty green **dental floss**. And all the kids in Room Nine **practice**d flossing.

Flossing is when you pull **string**s through your mouth.

Only pretty soon an **accident** happened.

That's because a boy named William **wind**ed his floss too tight. And his teeth and head got in a **tangled knot** ball. And Dr. Smiley couldn't **undo** him.

Then Mrs. had to call **Janitor speedy** quick. And so he runned to Room Nine. And he shined his giant **flashlight** in William's mouth.

And then Dr. Smiley got the dangerous floss right out of there!

Room Nine clapped and clapped.

Dr. Smiley did a **bow**.

Then Mrs. said that maybe some of us might like to **dress up** like dentists or police officers on Job Day.

"Yeah, only what if you don't like drunk guys or **bloody** teeth?" I asked.

Mrs. **roll**ed **her eyes** way up at the **ceiling**. Then she walked Officer Mike and Dr. Smiley out into the **hall**.

That's when Room Nine started **buzz**ing very loud.

Buzzing is what you do when your teacher leaves the room.

"I'm going to dress up like an actress on

Job Day," said a girl named Emily.

"I'm going to dress up like a princess," said my bestest friend Lucille that I hate.

I did a **giggle**. "I'm going to dress up like a **bullfighter!**" I said.

Then I ran speedy fast around the room. And I **butt**ed that **mean** Jim in the stomach with my head.

And guess what?

I didn't even get caught!

That's what!

3
Me and My Big Fat Mouth

After school was over, me and my bestest
friend named Grace walked to the bus
together.

Except for that Grace kept on wanting
to **skip**. And I didn't.

"How come you don't want to skip?"
she said. "Me and you always skip to the
bus."

"I know, Grace," I said. "But today I've

got a very big problem inside my head. And it's called I still don't know what job I want to be when I grow up."

"I do," said that Grace. "I'm going to be Mickey Mouse[1] at Disneyland.[2]"

I did a big **sigh** at her. "Yeah, only too bad for you, Grace," I said. "'Cause there's only one real alive Mickey Mouse. And you're not him."

That Grace laughed very hard.

"Mickey isn't *real*, **silly**. He's just a mouse **suit** with a guy inside," she said.

And so just then I felt very **sickish**

---

1 **Mickey Mouse** 미키 마우스. 미국의 유명 영화 제작사 디즈니 (Disney)가 만든 가장 대표적인 만화 주인공. 검고 둥근 귀를 지닌 쥐로 노란 단추가 달린 빨간 바지를 입은 것이 특징이다.

2 **Disneyland** 디즈니랜드. 미국 캘리포니아주(州) 남서부에 있는 세계 최고 수준의 유원지. 미국의 만화 영화 제작자 월트 디즈니(Walt Disney)가 계획하여 건축하였다.

inside of my stomach.

'Cause I didn't know Mickey was a suit, that's why.

"What did you have to tell me that for, Grace?" I said real **upset**. "Now I feel very **depress**ed."

Then I hurried up on the bus. And I **scoot**ed way **over** by the window.

Except I couldn't get any peace and

quiet. 'Cause everybody kept on talking about **dumb** old Job Day.

"I'm going to be a famous singer," said a girl named Rose.

"I'm going to be a famous **baton twirler,**³" said another girl named Lynnie.

Then a girl named Charlotte said she was going to be a famous painter. "Famous painters are called artists," she explained. "And artists are very rich."

After that I felt a little bit **cheerier.** 'Cause guess what? Grandma Miller says I paint beautifully, that's what.

"Hey. Maybe I'll be a famous painter

---

3 **baton twirler** 배턴 트월러. 행진이나 스포츠 경기에서 양 끝에 고무 추가 붙은 금속 봉인 배턴을 돌리거나 공중에 던지는 연기를 하는 사람을 말한다.

too," I said.

"I'm gonna be a **prison guard**," said a boy named Roger. "My uncle Roy is a prison guard. And he gets to carry the keys for the whole **entire** prison."

Then my mouth did a smile. 'Cause one time my dad gave me the key to the front door. And I un**lock**ed it all **by myself**. And I didn't even need any help!

"Hey. Maybe I might carry keys too, Roger," I said. "'Cause I know how to use those things very good."

Just then William raised his hand very **bashful**. "I'm going to be a superhero and save people from danger," he said.

And so then I jumped right out of my seat! 'Cause that was the bestest idea of all!

"Me too, William!" I **holler**ed. "'Cause that sounds very exciting, I think. And so I'm going to save people from danger too!"

Then that mean Jim jumped up at me. "**Copycat**! Copycat! You're just **copy**ing everybody else. And anyway, you can't be three jobs! You can only be one!"

I made a **growly** face at him.

"I *am* just being one job!" I said very angry. "It's a special kind of job where you paint and you unlock **stuff** and you save people! So there! Ha-ha on you!"

That Jim made a cuckoo **sign**[4] at me.

"Goonie,[5]" he said. "Goonie B. Jones.

---

4 **cuckoo sign** '미쳤다'라는 의미로 관자놀이 주변에서 손가락을 빙빙 돌리는 행동을 말한다.

There's no such job like that in the whole entire **universe!**"

"YES, THERE IS! THERE IS TOO, YOU BIG FAT JIM!" I **yell**ed. "AND IT'S THE BESTEST JOB IN THE WHOLE WIDE

---

5 goonie 바보나 꼴사나운 사람을 가리키는 표현으로, 여기에서는 짐이 주니(Junie) B.의 이름과 운을 맞추어 놀리기 위해 일부러 이 표현을 사용하였다.

WORLD!"

He **cross**ed **his arms** and did a mean
smile.

"Okay. Then what's the name of it?" he

said.

Then the bus got very quiet.

And everybody kept on waiting and waiting for me to say the name of my job.

Except for I just couldn't think of anything.

And so my face got very **reddish** and **hottish**.

And I felt like P.U. again.

"See? Told ja![6]" said that mean Jim. "There is no such job! Told ja! Told ja! Told ja!"

After that I sat down very quiet. And I **stare**d out the window.

'Cause the sickish feeling was back

---

6 **ja** 2인칭 인칭 대명사 'you(너, 당신)'의 비격식적인 축약형.

inside my stomach again, that's why.

Me and my big fat mouth.

4
Dumb Ollie

I got off the bus at my corner. Then I runned to my house **speedy** quick.

"HELP! HELP! I'M IN BIG TROUBLE!" I yelled to Mother. "'CAUSE I **ACCIDENTALLY** **SHOT OFF MY** BIG FAT **MOUTH** ON THE BUS! AND NOW I HAVE TO PAINT AND UN**LOCK** STUFF AND SAVE PEOPLE FROM DANGER! ONLY WHAT KIND OF STUPID DUMB

JOB IS THAT?"

"Back here," called Mother.

Back here means the **nursery**. The nursery is the place where my new baby brother named Ollie lives.

I ran there my very fastest.

Mother was **rock**ing Ollie in the rocking chair. He was a little bit sleeping.

"I NEED TO TALK TO YOU VERY BAD!" I shouted some more. "'CAUSE I DID A BIG **FIB**. AND NOW I DON'T KNOW HOW TO GET OUT OF IT!"

Just then Ollie waked up. He started crying very much.

"Great," said Mother very **growly**.

"Yeah, only sorry, but I'm **upset** here," I explained.

Ollie **screech**ed louder and louder. His voice sounded like a **scratchy sore throat**.

Mother put him on her **lap**. Then she **rub**bed the sides of her **forehead** with her fingers.

That's 'cause she had a mybrain **headache**,[1] I think.

"You're just going to have to wait until I get the baby **settle**d again," she said, still **grumpy**.

"Yeah, only I can't wait, 'cause—"

Mother **butt**ed **in**. "Not now, Junie B.! I'll be out to talk to you as soon as I can! Now please go!"

Then she pointed at the door.

---

1 **mybrain headache** 주니 B.가 'migraine headache(편두통)'을 잘못 알아듣고 말한 것이다.

Pointing means O-U-T.

"Darn it,[2]" I said. "Darn it, darn it, darn it."

'Cause that dumb old baby **takes up** all of Mother's time.

And he's not even interesting.

He doesn't know how to **roll** over. Or sit up. Or play Chinese checkers.[3]

He is a **dud**, I think.

I would like to take him back to the hospital. But Mother said no.

After I left the nursery, I went outside in my front **yard**.

---

2 **darn it** 'damn it(빌어먹을, 제기랄)'을 순화한 단어로, 못마땅하거나 짜증스러울 때 쓰는 속어적 표현.

3 **Chinese checkers** 차이니즈 체커 또는 다이아몬드 게임. 보드게임의 하나로 보통 2~3명이 하며, 다이아몬드 모양의 말판 위에서 자기 앞에 놓인 말을 건너편으로 먼저 모두 이동한 사람이 이기는 게임.

Then I sat in the grass all **by myself**.

And I played with a **stick** and another ant.

Only this stupid ant **bite**d me. And so I had to drop a rock on his head.

Finally my daddy's car came into the **driveway**. And my heart got very happy.

"Daddy's home! Daddy's home! **Hurray**! Hurray!" I yelled.

Then I ran to him. And he picked me up. And I gave him my most biggest[4] **hug**.

"I'm very glad to see you!" I said.

"'Cause on Monday I have to **dress up** like what job I want to be. **Except** for I accidentally said I'm going to paint and

---

4 **most biggest** 형용사 'big'의 최상급을 잘못 만든 것으로, 올바른 표현은 'biggest'이다. 이 책에 나오는 'funnest(most fun)', 'most beautifulest(most beautiful)' 등이 이와 같은 경우이다.

save people and carry lots of keys. Only
what kind of dumb bunny job is that?"

My daddy put me down. His **eyebrow**s
looked **confuse**d at me.

"Can we talk about this at dinner? he
asked.

"No," I said. "We have to talk right
now. 'Cause I've already waited all I can.
And I'm getting **tension** in me."

"Well, I'm afraid you're just going to
have to wait a little while longer," said
Daddy. "Because right now I've got to see if
your mother needs help with the baby."

Then he did a kiss on my head. And he
walked right into the house!

And guess what?

Sometimes I wish stupid dumb Ollie

never even came to live with us.

5
Shining

When I went back inside, Ollie was still very **scream**ing.

That's 'cause Mother couldn't find his **pacifier**.

Pacifiers are what babies like to **suck** on. Except I don't know why. 'Cause one time I sucked on Ollie's. And it tasted like my red **sneaker**s.

Just then Mother runned out of Ollie's

room.

And her hair was very **stick**ing out.

And her clothes were all **wrinkly**.

And she was wearing one sock, and **that's all**.

"WHERE IS IT? WHERE IS THE PACIFIER? IT JUST DIDN'T **DISAPPEAR** INTO THIN AIR, YOU KNOW!" she **holler**ed very loud.

Then me and Daddy had to help Mother look for the pacifier speedy quick. 'Cause she was losing her **grip**, I think.

I looked in the **couch**. That's because sometimes if you push your hand way under the cushions, you can find some good **stuff** under there.

This time I found three Cheetos[1] and a

popcorn.

They were very delicious.

After that, I looked under Daddy's big chair. Only it was too dark to see under there. And so I runned to get the **flashlight**. 'Cause I learned about flashlights in school, remember?

Flashlights are fun to shine in the dark. I shined it in the dark **closet**. And also down the dark **basement** steps.

Then I remembered another dark place. And its name was screaming Ollie's room. 'Cause his **shade**s were pulled down for his **nap**, that's why.

I runned right there very fast.

---

1 **Cheetos** 치토스. 1948년 미국에서 출시되어 지금까지 전 세계적으로 판매되는 과자. 주황색으로 치즈 맛이 나는 것이 특징이다.

"Look," I said to screaming Ollie. "I've got a flashlight."

I shined it on his **ceiling**.

"See? See that little round circle of shine up there?" I said.

Then I shined it on his **jungle wallpaper**.

"And see the monkeys, Ollie? And the hippo-pot-of-something?[2]" I asked him.

Only screaming Ollie just kept right on screaming. And he didn't show **courtesy** to me.

Courtesy is the school word for listening very **polite**.

That's how come I shined it right in his

---

2 **hippo-pot-of-something** 주니 B.가 'hippopotamus(하마)'라는 단어가 완전히 기억나지 않아 얼버무린 말.

big fat crying mouth.

Except for just then a problem happened. And it's called Mother **sneak**ed up on me in her quiet sock.

"JUNIE B. JONES! WHAT IN THE WORLD DO YOU THINK YOU'RE DOING?" she hollered.

I did a **gulp**. Then my heart got very **pump**y.³ Because I was in big trouble, that's why.

"I'm shinin'," I said real soft.

"OUT!" she said. "OUT RIGHT NOW!"

And so that's how come I started to leave. Except for then the flashlight shined

---

3 **pumpy** 주니 B.가 만들어 낸 단어로 동사 'pump(아래위로 빠르게 움직이다)'의 뒤에 '-y'를 붙여 '빠르게 움직이는' 또는 '쿵쾅대는'이라는 의미의 형용사로 사용하였다.

on the floor. And I saw something very wonderful down there.

"HEY! LOOK! IT'S THE PACIFIER!" I shouted. "I FOUND THE PACIFIER! IT WAS HIDING UNDER THE **ROCK**ING CHAIR!"

Then I hurried to pick it up. And I gave it to Mother.

Her face got **relief** on it.

"**Thank goodness**," she said.

"Yes. Thank goodness," I said back.

Mother **wipe**d the pacifier off. Then she **blow**ed on it very hard.

"Yeah, only you can't blow **germ**s off, you know," I said. "'Cause stuff that's been on the ground is very dangerous."

And so then Mother gave me the

pacifier. And I washed it off with soap and water.

And guess what? Then I put it right in Ollie's mouth. And he stopped crying!

Mother looked **proud** of me.

"Where did you get so smart?" she asked.

"At school, that's where," I said.

Then **all of a sudden** my eyes got big and wide. 'Cause a very great idea **pop**ped right inside of my head!

"HEY! I THOUGHT OF IT!" I hollered. "I THOUGHT OF WHAT I CAN BE FOR JOB DAY!"

Then I jumped up and down. And I runned down the **hall**.

Daddy was in his chair reading the

paper.

I **bust**ed through it with my head.

"I THOUGHT OF IT! I THOUGHT OF WHAT KIND OF JOB I CAN BE WHEN I GROW UP!"

Daddy said, "Slow down," to me. That's because he didn't know what the heck I was talking about, of course.

"Yeah, only I can't slow down," I explained. "'Cause I'm very **celebrating**! And now I don't have **tension** in me anymore!"

Just then Mother came into the room.

"What's all the excitement about?" she said.

I **clap**ped my hands together. "I have a '**nounce**ment, that's what it's all about!" I said real happy.

"Well, what is it?" said Mother. "Tell us!"

And so then I stood up straight and tall.

And I told Mother and Daddy the name of the job I'm going to be when I grow up!

"That's a good one, right?" I said very excited. "That's the bestest job you ever heard of, isn't it?"

Except for Mother and Daddy didn't answer me. They just kept on looking and looking at each other.

Then Daddy did a funny smile.

And Mother said the word *ho boy.*[4]

---

4 **boy** 여기에서는 '소년'이라는 뜻이 아니라, '맙소사' 또는 '어머나'라는 의미로 놀람이나 기쁨 등을 나타내는 표현으로 쓰였다.

6
Tingling

I couldn't sleep for the whole weekend.
That's because I had tingling excitement in
me about Job Day. And my brain wouldn't
settle down.

And so on Monday, I **zoom**ed to the
bus stop very fast.

"Look, Mr. Woo!" I said to my bus
driver. "Look what I'm wearing today!"

Then I opened my jacket and I showed

him my job clothes.

"See? It's nice pants. And **dangling** keys. And a paint**brush**," said. "**Except** for I can't tell you what I am, 'cause it's my special secret."

Then I **plop**ped down in my seat. And me and Mr. Woo drove to the next corner.

That's where my bestest friend Grace got on.

She was wearing Mickey Mouse ears and a dress with red and white **polka dot**ties on it!

"Grace!" I said very smiling. "You look very beautiful in that dotty thing."

"I know it," she said. "That's because I changed my mind about who I'm going to be when I grow up. Now I'm going to be

Minnie[1] **instead** of Mickey."

Then I stopped smiling. And my
stomach felt very **sickish** inside again.

'Cause that meant Minnie Mouse was a

---

1 **Minnie** (= Minnie Mouse) 미니 마우스. 미국의 유명 영화 제작사 디
즈니(Disney)가 만든 미키 마우스(Mickey Mouse)의 여자친구. 주로 물
방울무늬의 옷을 입고 머리에는 리본을 달고 있는 것이 특징이다.

fake too.

"Disneyland is a **fib**," I said.

After that, the bus stopped again. And William got on.

He was wearing a Superman **outfit**. Except he had a W on the front of him. And not the letter S.

"The W **stands for** William," he said to
Mr. Woo.

"Does that mean you can fly?" asked
Mr. Woo.

Then William **grin**ned very big. And
he held out his arms. And he jumped way
high in the air.

Except for he didn't fly.

And so he just sat down.

After that, other kids got on the bus,
too.

And Roger had on keys just like me.
And also plastic **handcuffs**.

And Charlotte was wearing a red
paint **apron** with some **watercolors** in the
pocket.

And that **mean** Jim was wearing a white

bathrobe.

"Hey! I've got a bathrobe just like that, Jim!" I said very **friendly.**

"It's not a bathrobe, **dummy,**" he said. "I'm a kung fu^2 karate^3 guy."

"Jim is a kung fu karate guy," I said to Grace. "Except for he just got out of the **bathtub.**"

Then me and her laughed and laughed. 'Cause that was a funny **joke,** of course.

And Job Day was going to be the funnest day in the whole wide world!

---

2 **kung fu** 쿵후. 중국 무술의 하나로 무기 없이 손과 발을 이용하는 권법.
3 **karate** 가라테. 일본 무술의 하나로 무기를 쓰지 않고 맨손으로 하는 권법. 차기, 치기, 찌르기의 세 방법이 기본을 이룬다.

7
Jobs and Jobs

When I got off the bus, I **zoom**ed to Room Nine. That's because I wanted Job Day to start very quick.

Only first we had to take **attendance**.

And then we had to say *I pledge allegiance to the flag of the United States of America, and to the republic for which it stands.*[1]

Except I don't know what that **dumb**

story is even talking about.

Then finally Mrs. **clap**ped her loud hands together.

And guess what? Job Day started, that's what!

"Boys and girls, you all look wonderful in your **outfit**s!" Mrs. said. "I can't wait to learn what all of you want to be when you grow up! Who would like to go first?"

"I WOULD! I WOULD!" I **yell**ed out.

Only then my bestest friend Lucille raised her hand very **polite**. And she got to go first.

Lucille looked the most beautifulest I've ever seen her.

---

1 **I pledge allegiance . . . which it stands** 미국의 국기에 대한 맹세. 우리나라에서 하듯이 오른손을 왼쪽 가슴 위에 얹고 말한다.

She was wearing a new dress that her **nanna** bought for her. It was the color of pink velvet.[2]

Also she had on **shiny** pink shoes. And socks with **bow**s and lace on them.

Lucille's nanna is **load**ed, I think.

Lucille went to the front of the room. She **reach**ed into a little bag and pulled out a **sparkling crown** with **jewel**s on it!

Then all of Room Nine said, "Oooooh."

Except for not the boys.

"When I grow up, I'm going to marry a prince," she said. "And I'll be a princess. And my name will be Princess Lucille."

Then she put the sparkling crown on

---

2 **velvet** 벨벳. 짧고 부드러운 솜털이 광택을 내는 고급 원단.

her head. And she looked like a **fairy tale** guy.

Mrs. smiled. "That's a **lovely** thought, Lucille," she said.

"I know," said Lucille. "My nanna says if

you marry a prince, you're **set for life**."

After that, Lucille said her dress costed eighty-five. And her shoes costed forty-five. And her **lacy** socks costed six fifty plus **tax**.

Then Mrs. told Lucille to sit down.

Ricardo went next.

He was wearing a round yellow hat. It was the kind of hat you can **bang** on.

"This is called a hard hat,[3]" he said. "You have to wear it when you're building tall buildings. Or else somebody might drop a **hammer** from way up high. And it could hit you on the head and kill you."

Mrs. smiled. "So you're interested in

---

3 **hard hat** 안전모. 공장이나 작업장 또는 운동 경기 등에서 머리가 다치는 것을 막기 위하여 쓰는 모자.

construction, right, Ricardo?" she asked.

But Ricardo just kept on talking about other **stuff** that could fall on your head and kill you. Like a paint can. And an **electric drill**. And a lunchbox.

Then Mrs. said, "Sit down," to him, too.

That's when William raised his hand. Only he was being very **bashful**. And he wouldn't go to the front of the room.

"You don't have to be nervous, William," said Mrs. "Just tell us what you want to be when you grow up."

William **cover**ed his face with his hands.

"Super William," he said very quiet.

Then he got out of his seat. And he jumped way high in the air. Only his

cape got **tangle**d up in his chair. And he **crash**ed into the table.

After that, Super William got very **sniffling**. And Mrs. said we would get back to him later.

Then lots of other kids talked about their jobs.

Like a boy named Clifton is going to be a rich and famous **astronaut**.

And a girl named Lily is going to be a rich and famous movie star. And also she wants to **direct**.

And a boy named Ham is going to be a rich and famous boss of a big company. And he taught us how to say the word *you're* **fired**.

And here's the bestest one of all! 'Cause

a boy named Jamal Hall is going to be the rich and famous **president** of the whole United States!

"Cool!" said Ricardo.

Then the other boys said, "Cool," too.

I did a secret smile. Yeah, only not as cool as my job, I thought to just myself.

Then I raised my hand very polite. And Mrs. called my name.

"OH, BOY!" I shouted. "OH, BOY! OH, BOY! 'CAUSE MINE IS EVEN BETTER THAN PRESIDENT OF THE UNITED STATES!"

I zoomed **speedy** quick to the front of the room.

Then my excitement wouldn't stay inside of me anymore.

"A **JANITOR**! I'M GOING TO BE A JANITOR!" I **holler**ed out.

After that, I **jingle**d my **jangly** keys! And I **wave**d my paint**brush** in the air! And I clapped and clapped!

Only too bad for me.

'Cause nobody clapped back.

And here's something even worser.[4]

Room Nine started laughing very much. And it was the **mean** kind.

"SHE WANTS TO BE A JANITOR!" they yelled.

Then they pointed at my brown pants.

And they called me the name of stupid.

And I didn't know what to do. 'Cause I

---

4 **worser** 형용사 'bad'의 비교급을 잘못 만든 것으로, 올바른 표현은 'worse'이다.

felt very **crumbling** inside.

And so I just kept on standing there and standing there.

And my eyes got a little bit of wet in them. And my nose started running very much.

That's how come I covered my face up.

"They're not having **courtesy** for me," I said real soft.

Only just then Mrs. clapped her angry hands together. And she **scold**ed Room Nine a real lot.

"Junie B. is right," she said. "Being a janitor is a very important job. You have to be **hardworking** and **reliable** and very, very **trustworthy**."

I **peek**ed through my fingers at her.

"Yeah, and don't forget the part where you have to save people from danger," I said.

Then that Jim I hate laughed right out loud. "Janitors don't save people from danger, you goonie bird!" he said.

I **stamp**ed my foot at him. "Yes, they do! They do too! Because one time I was eating a dangerous Life Saver. And Janitor made me **spit** it out! And also he brought his **flashlight** to Room Nine. And he saved William from the dangerous **dental floss**!"

Then I held up my jingling keys.

"And see these things? Keys are what Janitor un**lock**s the bathroom door with. Or else we couldn't even go to the **toilet**!"

Then I showed him my paintbrush.

"And Janitor paints **litter** cans, too," I said. "And painting is the funnest thing I love!"

That Jim did a mean smile. "Yeah, well, too bad for you, but you're a girl. And janitors have to be boys. So there."

I runned to his table. "No, they do not, you stupid head Jim!" I said. "Girls can be anything boys can be! Right, Mrs.? Right? Right? 'Cause I saw that on *Sesame Street.*[5] And also on *Oprah.*[6]"

Mrs. did a smile.

Then my bestest friend Grace started to

---

5 **Sesame Street** 세서미 스트리트. 1969년에 미국에서 처음 방영되어 현재는 전 세계에서 사랑받는 3~5세 유아를 위한 교육 TV 프로그램이다. '엘모', '쿠키 몬스터', '머핏' 등의 인형들이 나오는 것이 특징이다.

6 **Oprah** 오프라 윈프리(Oprah Winfrey) 쇼. 미국의 가장 유명한 방송인 중 한 사람인 오프라 윈프리가 진행한 토크쇼. 1986년부터 2011년까지 25년 동안 미국을 비롯한 140여개국에 방영되었다.

clap.

And guess what? All of the other girls in Room Nine clapped too.

8
Gus Vallony

Today **Janitor** came to Room Nine for Show and Tell![1]

And it was the funnest day I ever saw!

That's 'cause he brought his very big **tool**box with him.

And we played a game called Name the

---

1 **show and tell** 유치원이나 초등학교에서 주로 하는 수업 활동의 하나로, 학생들이 각자 자신에게 의미 있는 물건을 가지고 와서 그것에 대해 발표하는 시간이다.

Tools.

And guess what?

I knew the **saw**.

And the **hammer**.

And the **metric** socket² set with **adjustable** ratchet.³

Then Janitor showed us how to use his **stuff**.

And Charlotte got to shine his **giant flashlight**.

And my bestest friend Grace got to push his big **broom**.

And lucky duck⁴ Lucille got to clean the

---

2 **socket** 내부의 모양과 그 크기가 다른 원통형의 속이 빈 공구.
3 **ratchet** 래칫. 흔히 우리가 소켓 렌치라고 부르는 것으로, 핸들에 소켓을 꽂아 넣고 육각 볼트나 육각 너트를 풀거나 조일 때 사용하는 공구이다.
4 **lucky duck** 굉장히 운이 좋은 사람을 이르는 말.

chalkboard with his **squishy** sponge.

Except for then a little bit of trouble happened. 'Cause I wanted the **mop**. Only that stupid head Jim wouldn't **let go of** it. And so I had to **pinch** his arm.

After that, the mop got **remove**d from us.

Removed is the school word for **snatch**ed right out of our hands.

After that, Janitor sat in a chair. And Room Nine sat all around him.

Then he told us all about himself and his job.

And guess what?

He's been Janitor for fourteen years.

And he was borned in a different country from ours.

And his name is Gus Vallony!

"Hey! I love that name of Gus Vallony!" I **holler**ed out. "'Cause Vallony[5] is my favorite kind of sandwich!"

Then I smiled very **proud**.

"And guess what else?" I said to Room Nine. "Me and Janitor are bestest friends. And sometimes he calls me the **nickname** of sis!"

Then Janitor **wink**ed at me.

And so I winked back. Except for both my eyes kept on shutting. And so I had to hold one of them open with my fingers.

"I really like that Gus Vallony,"

---

5 **Vallony** 여기에서는 주니 B.가 경비원의 이름인 Vallony를 'baloney (볼로냐소시지)'라고 잘못 알아듣고 말한 것이다. 볼로냐소시지는 곱게 다져 절인 돼지고기나 쇠고기를 섞어 훈제하고 익힌 음식이다.

I **whisper**ed to my bestest friend Lucille.

Only then that **dumb** girl named Lily heard what I said.

And she started singing, *"Junie B's got a boyyy friennnd. Junie B's got a boyyy*

friennnd."

And so that's how come I felt very **embarrass**ed.

"Me and my big fat mouth!" I said.

Then Mrs. laughed.

And Janitor laughed.

And everybody else laughed too.

After that, Janitor had to go back to work. And so Mrs. shook his hand.

Then Room Nine **clap**ped and clapped for him.

And Janitor smiled.

And his **jingly** keys **jangle**d all the way out the door.